COOKERY

▨ A PROJECT BOOK

PROJECT
BOOK
059

Make your own Bread and Cakes

D1764780

By Maureen O'Connor
Illustrated by Ken Williams

PUBLISHED BY PETER HADDOCK LTD
BRIDLINGTON - ENGLAND

exclusive to
WOOLWORTH + WOOLCO

PART ONE

Bread—a basic food

How many times a day do you eat bread? You almost certainly have a slice at breakfast, either fried or toasted, and perhaps a piece with soup for lunch or a slice or two at teatime with jam or honey. In fact bread is one of your basic foods. You eat more of it than almost anything else.

Although it is such an important part of our diet, bread is a very complicated food to prepare and it took men thousands of years to discover all the various processes which change a few grains of wheat into the bread you eat. If you look at a grain of wheat it may seem almost impossible that it could ever become bread at all, because it is so hard and unappetising.

Wheat grains have to be milled in order to turn them into flour. This process is a great deal more difficult than it looks. It took prehistoric man thousands of years to discover that he could grind down the seeds of various common grasses into flour or meal which he could eat. You might try crushing some wheat grains in a pestle and mortar if you want to discover just how hard it is.

Some time about four thousand years ago primitive men discovered that grains of wheat, or other types of corn, could be ground between two stones. At first they held the stones between their hands. Then, gradually, they developed large millstones which could be moved, one on top of the other, turned either by men or by an animal such as the donkey, or later on, by the wind in various forms of windmill.

With the invention of large scale machinery, it became possible to grind corn without the aid of the wind, and flour mills now look very much like any other large factory, though perhaps a bit more dusty. There may still be a windmill in your area, or the site of an old windmill. If so see how long it is since it stopped grinding corn for the local bakers. You may also find that there is a flour mill locally, especially if you live near a river or sea port. Before you start to make bread, why not try to find out just where your flour has come from. It may have had a longer journey than you expect.

Yeast

Even when primitive men had discovered how to grind corn it took them much longer to learn how to make bread as we know it. At first they simply mixed their flour with water and baked it on hot stones or in a simple stone oven. This gave them a flat, crisp, rather uninteresting cake of *unleavened* bread, that is, bread which has not had anything added to its mixture to make it rise. This is the type of bread which is mentioned in the Bible and which Jews still eat when celebrating their religious feasts.

But the Jews, as the Bible shows, did know how to make a *leavened*, or lightened bread, which rose when it was cooked, and it is believed that they learnt to add yeast to their bread mixture from the Egyptians, who had been using it about 3,000 years before Christ. Yeast is a microscopic plant which lives on sugar. If the yeast is given sugar to eat in warm, moist conditions, it will grow. As it grows and multiplies it gives off a gas, carbon dioxide, and it is this gas which swells and makes the dough light and spongy. Naturally most people prefer a light,

Fig. 1

spongy bread to a hard and rather indigestible one, so once it had been discovered that yeast made bread rise, the method spread from the Jews to the Greeks and then the Romans. As the Romans conquered Europe in the first centuries after Christ they brought with them this improved method of making bread.

PROJECT

The history of bread

How far back can you trace the history of bread making? Does anyone in your family remember when all their bread was made at home? Does anyone in your family still make bread? Is there a bakery near where you live where bread is still made on the premises? Is there a large bakery which supplies several shops? Where does the flour for the bakery come from? Where does the grain come from before it reaches the flour mill? Is there a windmill, or the site of a windmill, near your home? In times past, was bread a food eaten mainly by the rich or the poor? What were the Corn Laws? Does Britain import corn to make bread? Can you discover how bread was made in Elizabethan times? Or in Saxon times? Or in Roman times? As far as we know the Egyptians were the first people to use yeast to leaven bread. Can you discover how we know this, and what else they used yeast for?

How yeast works

Yeast is a microscopic plant and you must remember that it is alive. If it is to grow and work to produce the gas which will make your dough rise it must have the conditions it likes to live and work in. It must have:

Fresh air. Like human beings, yeast grows best when there is plenty of oxygen about.

Food. Yeast lives on sugar and when making bread doughs it is usual to give the yeast a teaspoonful of sugar to start off its growth. It then lives on the sugars which are in the flour itself.

Warmth. Yeast will not grow if it is too hot or too cold, so it is very important, when making bread, to have the mixing bowl and ingredients warm and to work in a warm room. The ideal temperature at which yeast will work best is about blood heat, 98.4 °F. Too much heat will kill yeast, and too little warmth will stop it growing.

If you remember that yeast is a sensitive plant and needs all these conditions, you should have no difficulty in making a good, light loaf of bread. Some substances kill yeast or stop it working. These are salt, chocolate and cocoa powders, oil of lemon, turpentine and strong alcohol.

OTHER POINTS TO REMEMBER

1 Remember that when yeast is rising in a dough it is a plant growing. You cannot hurry it. If a recipe tells you to leave the dough for 1 hour, it really means 1 hour. So if you want to make bread, leave yourself plenty of time. Perhaps you can find something else to do while the dough is rising.

2 You may be able to obtain fresh yeast from the baker, and these recipes give the correct quantities for fresh yeast. But if you cannot obtain fresh yeast, then it is quite all right to use dried yeast from a packet or tin. Normally you should use half the amount of dried yeast, but read the instructions on the tin or packet carefully.

3 The yeast will make little gas bubbles in the dough and it is important that these should be spread evenly throughout your loaf. This is the main reason for kneading the dough thoroughly, so do not cut down the time allowed for this. Knead very thoroughly and then cut the dough in two to make sure that the bubbles are evenly distributed.

PROJECT

Make a plain white loaf

You need: 1 pound flour, $\frac{1}{2}$ ounce yeast, $\frac{1}{2}$ level teaspoonful sugar, $\frac{1}{2}$ pint lukewarm water, 1 level teaspoonful salt.

What to do

1 Sift the flour and salt into a mixing bowl and warm.

2 Cream the yeast and sugar together in a jug until liquid and add the lukewarm water.

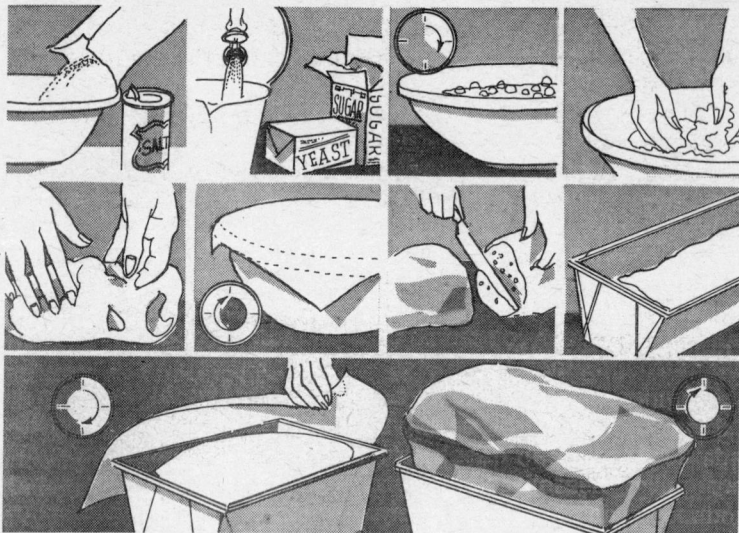

Fig. 2

3 Make a well in the centre of the flour and pour in the yeast mixture. Sprinkle a little flour over the top of the liquid and leave the bowl in a warm place for about 20 minutes until the surface is covered with bubbles.

4 Work in all the flour by hand, using a little more warm water if necessary to make a stiff dough.

5 Turn the dough on to a board and knead very thoroughly for 5 minutes to spread the yeast through the dough.

6 Put the dough in a clean floured bowl, cover with a cloth and leave to stand in a warm place for about an hour or until the dough has grown to twice its original size.

7 Turn the dough onto the board and knead again to make sure the air bubbles are evenly distributed. Cut the dough in half to check.

8 Shape the dough into a loaf shape and put into a greased loaf tin. It should half fill the tin, to allow for rising.

9 Cover with a cloth and leave to stand in a warm place for about 30 minutes, or until the dough has risen to the top of the tin.

10 Bake in a ready heated oven for about 1 hour (Gas Mark 6 or electric 400°F) until the crust is brown and the loaf sounds hollow when tapped on the base.

Variation: bread rolls

Follow the recipe for white bread up to stage 7. Then divide the dough into 8 or 12 equal sized pieces and shape each one into a roll shape, a plait or a twist. Place the rolls on a greased baking tray, cover with a cloth and leave them in a warm place for about 15 minutes until they double in size. Brush them with milk and bake for 15 to 20 minutes in a ready heated oven (Gas Mark 6 or electric 400°F).

PROJECT

Make a brown loaf

You need: 1 pound wholemeal flour, ½ ounce yeast, ½ level teaspoonful sugar, ¾ ounce butter, ½ pint lukewarm water, 1 level teaspoonful salt.

What to do

1 Sift the flour and salt into a mixing bowl and warm.

2 Rub the butter into the flour until the mixture looks like fine breadcrumbs.

3 Cream the yeast and sugar together in a jug until liquid and add the water.

4 Make a well in the centre of the flour and pour in the yeast mixture. Sprinkle a little flour over the top of the liquid and leave the bowl in a warm place for about 20 minutes until the surface is covered in bubbles.

5 Continue to make the bread according to the recipe for white bread above from point 4.

This dough can also be made into small rolls.

PROJECT

Make milk bread

You need: 1 pound flour, $\frac{1}{2}$ ounce yeast, $\frac{1}{2}$ teaspoonful sugar, 2 ounces butter, 1 level teaspoonful salt, $\frac{1}{2}$ pint warm milk, 1 egg. (This makes a richer and softer loaf than the basic bread recipe.)

Fig. 3

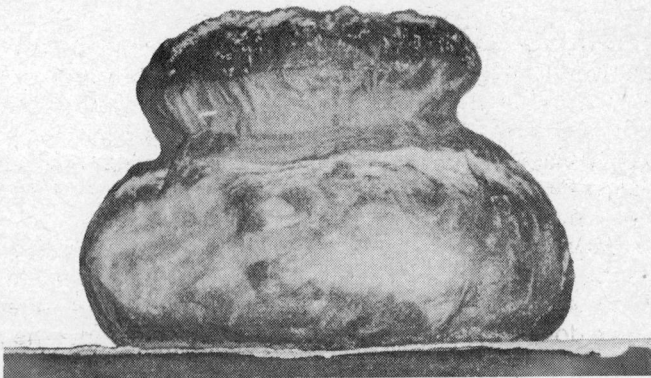

What to do

1 Sift the flour and salt into a mixing bowl and warm.

2 Cream the yeast and sugar together with a tablespoonful of milk.

3 Rub the butter into the flour until the mixture looks like fine breadcrumbs.

4 Mix in the yeast, milk and egg to make a soft, light dough.

5 Beat this dough with a fork or electric beater until it is smooth and leaves the sides of the bowl clean and dry.

6 Continue to make the bread by following the recipe for a white loaf from point 6.

Variations

1. Rolls. This dough can also be used to make soft rolls, or bridge rolls, which should be made in a thin sausage shape and baked touching each other on the baking tray so that the sides stay soft.

2. Currant loaves. Follow the recipe above, and before making the dough into a loaf shape work in 2 ounces of currants and 1 ounce of finely chopped candied peel.

3. Cottage loaf (*fig. 3*). Follow the recipe above and when the dough is ready for shaping divide it into two pieces, one twice as big as the other. Make the larger piece of dough into the shape of a round bun and make the smaller piece into a similar, smaller shape. Put the smaller piece of dough on top of the larger piece and push a finger through the centre of the two pieces to make them stick together.

4. Plaited loaf (*figs. 4–8*). Follow the recipe above and when the dough is ready for shaping divide it into three. Shape each piece into a long thin roll and plait the pieces together. Stick the dough at the ends of the loaf together so that the plait cannot come undone.

You will find that you can make other large and small fancy loaves with this dough. They can be brushed with milk or an egg and milk mixture if you want a glossy crust on the loaf or roll.

Fig. 4

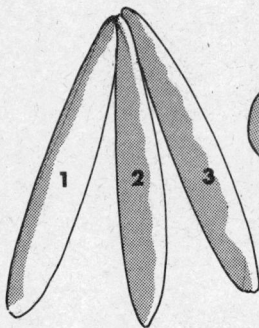

Fig. 5

Fig. 6

Fig. 7

Fig. 8

PART TWO

Breads at home and away

Because it is such a basic food there is a very wide variety of types of bread. Nearly every country has its own variation on the plain loaf and this section gives some recipes for breads from Britain and abroad. You might find it interesting to discover if any of these breads are eaten at any special time of day in their native countries. And when you have tried them all, see if you can find even more recipes for breads from different parts of the world.

PROJECT

Make Vienna bread [*fig. 9 (1)*]

You need: 1 pound flour, 1 level teaspoonful salt, $\frac{1}{2}$ ounce yeast, 1 level teaspoonful caster sugar, 1 ounce butter, $\frac{1}{2}$ pint lukewarm milk, 1 egg.

What to do

1 Sift the flour and salt into a mixing bowl and warm.

2 Cream the yeast and sugar together.

3 Melt the butter over a low heat and add most of the milk.

4 Lightly beat the egg and add the butter and milk and the yeast. Mix well.

Fig. 9

5 Make a well in the centre of the flour and add the yeast mixture. Mix to a soft dough, adding a little more milk if necessary. Knead the mixture thoroughly with the hands.

6 Cover the bowl with a cloth and leave the dough in a warm place for about an hour until it has doubled in size.

7 Knead the dough again on a floured board and divide it into two. Make each piece into a thick roll, wider at the centre than at the ends. Put the rolls onto a greased baking tray and mark the top with three diagonal slits with a sharp knife.

8 Leave the rolls for about 15 minutes until they have doubled in size.

9 Brush the tops with beaten egg and bake in a hot oven (Gas Mark 7, electric 425°F) for 20 minutes.

PROJECT How to make Irish soda bread

This bread is made without yeast. The bicarbonate of soda in the dough forms the gas bubbles which make the bread rise.

You need: 1 pound plain flour, 1 level teaspoonful salt, 1 level teaspoonful bicarbonate of soda, ½ pint buttermilk.

What to do

1 Sift together the flour, salt and bicarbonate of soda.

2 Mix in the buttermilk to make a soft dough.

3 Knead the dough lightly and make it into a large round cake.

4 Put the bread on a floured baking tray. Cut three diagonal lines across the top with a sharp knife and prick with a fork all over.

5 Bake in a hot oven for about 30 minutes (Gas Mark 7, electric 425°F).

If buttermilk is unobtainable, you can still make soda bread with the same amount of sour milk, in which case you should rub 1 ounce of butter into the flour, OR with fresh milk, in which case you should rub 1 ounce of butter into the flour and add 1 heaped teaspoonful of cream of tartar to the dry ingredients.

PROJECT

Make French croissants [*fig. 9 (2)*]

You need: 1 pound plain flour, ½ level teaspoonful salt, ½ ounce yeast, 1 level teaspoonful sugar, ½ pint warm milk and water, 3 ounces butter.

What to do

1 Sift the flour and salt together in a mixing bowl and warm.

2 Cream the yeast and sugar together.

3 Make a well in the centre of the flour and mix in the yeast and milk and water to make a soft, light dough.

4 Beat the mixture with a fork or electric beater until the dough is smooth and leaves the side of the basin clean.

5 Cover the bowl with a cloth and leave to stand in a warm place, until the dough has grown to twice its original size.

6 When the dough has risen, put it on a floured board and roll it out flat until it is about three times as wide.

7 Divide the butter into three and spread one third of it over the dough. Sprinkle lightly with flour and fold the dough in onto itself, one third up and one third down, and seal the edges, by pressing them firmly together.

8 Repeat this process twice to use up the other two pieces of butter. Then put the dough in a warm place again to rise for another 30 minutes.

9 Roll the dough out on a floured board until it is about $\frac{1}{8}$ in. thick.

10 Cut it into 12 square pieces. Turn each square over and damp it lightly with warm water.

11 Then roll each square up gently from one corner to the opposite corner using a little water to make the final corner stick down to the roll. Turn the ends of each roll in to make a half-moon shape.

12 Leave the croissants on a greased tray for a further 15 minutes to rise. Then bake in a hot oven (Gas Mark 7, electric 425°F) for about 20 minutes until they are crisp.

13 When they are light brown in colour brush the tops with a mixture of milk and beaten egg yolk and return them to the oven to dry off.

Make Italian grisini sticks [*fig. 9 (3)*]

You need: 1 pound plain flour, 1 level teaspoonful salt, 1 ounce butter, ½ ounce yeast, ½ level teaspoonful sugar, ½ pint warm milk.

What to do

1 Make a bread dough, following the recipe for milk bread and allow the dough to rise for 1 to 1½ hours.

2 Shape the dough into long thin sticks about 8 in. long.

3 Put the sticks on a greased baking tray and leave in a warm place until they have doubled in size.

4 Brush with milk and sprinkle with cooking salt and then bake in a hot oven (Gas Mark 7, electric 425 °F) until crisp.

PART THREE

With a spoonful of sugar

Yeast is not just used in bread. Some yeast doughs are used to make sweet buns and cakes and delicious sweets like rum babas. Here is a selection of recipes for sweet dishes using yeast. Perhaps when you have tried these you can discover others. Once you have learnt to use yeast in these basic recipes you will know how to handle it on any occasion.

PROJECT

Make Hot Cross Buns for Easter (*fig. 10*)

These are the buns traditionally eaten on Good Friday and marked with a cross in memory of the crucifixion of Jesus Christ. This year why not make Hot Cross Buns at home for your family.

You need: 1 pound plain flour, 1 level teaspoonful salt, 1 level teaspoonful mixed spice, 1 level teaspoonful cinnamon, 2 ounces butter, 2 ounces currants, 1 ounce yeast, $1\frac{1}{2}$ ounces sugar, $\frac{1}{2}$ pint warm milk.

What to do

1 Sift together the flour, salt, spice and cinnamon and rub in the butter until the mixture looks like fine breadcrumbs.

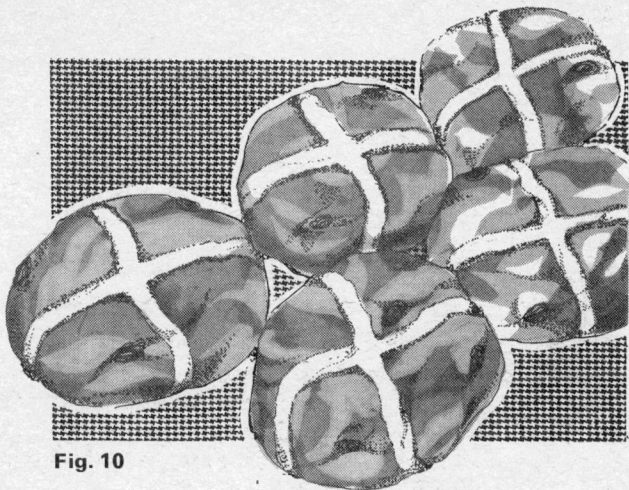
Fig. 10

2 Mix in the currants and put the bowl to warm.

3 Cream the yeast and sugar together until liquid and add the milk. Leave in a warm place for 10 minutes.

4 Make a well in the centre of the flour and mix in the yeast to make a soft dough. Beat together thoroughly.

5 Cover the bowl and leave it in a warm place until the dough has doubled in size.

6 Turn it onto a floured board and divide it into 12 equal pieces.

7 Shape the pieces into buns and mark each with a cross, cutting in deeply with a sharp knife.

8 Put the buns onto a greased baking tray and leave in a warm place for about 20 minutes until they have doubled in size.

9 Bake for 20 minutes in a hot oven (Gas Mark 6, electric 400°F).

10 When you take the buns out of the oven brush the tops with a little sugar dissolved in warm water.

PROJECT

Make Bath buns

You need: 1 pound plain flour, 1 level teaspoonful salt, 4 ounces butter, 1 ounce yeast, 4 ounces sugar, 3 eggs, 2 ounces sultanas, 2 ounces chopped candied peel, a little warm milk, grated lemon rind.

What to do

1 Sift together the flour and salt and rub in the butter until the mixture looks like fine breadcrumbs. Put the bowl to warm.

2 Cream the yeast with one teaspoonful of the sugar.

3 Beat the eggs and add enough warm milk to make $\frac{1}{2}$ pint of liquid. Add this to the yeast.

4 Pour the yeast mixture into the flour and beat together for about 5 minutes until the dough is very smooth.

5 Cover the bowl with a cloth and leave in a warm place until the dough has doubled in size.

6 Turn onto a floured board and knead in the remaining sugar, lemon rind, sultanas and peel.

7 Divide the dough into 12 pieces and form them into buns.

8 Put the buns onto a greased baking tray and leave in a warm place for about 20 minutes, until they have doubled in size.

9 Dissolve a little sugar in warm water and brush this over the top of the buns. Sprinkle with more sugar and bake in a hot oven (Gas Mark 6, electric 400°F) for 20 minutes.

Make Chelsea buns

You need: 8 ounces flour, $\frac{1}{2}$ level teaspoonful salt, 2 ounces butter, $\frac{1}{2}$ ounce yeast, 2 ounces caster sugar, 1 egg, about $\frac{1}{4}$ pint warm milk, 1 ounce chopped candied peel, 1 ounce sultanas, 1 ounce currants. For the glaze: white of egg and caster sugar.

What to do

1 Sift together the flour and the salt and rub in 1 ounce of the butter until the mixture looks like fine breadcrumbs. Put the bowl to warm.

2 Cream the yeast with one teaspoonful of sugar.

3 Beat the egg and add enough warm milk to make $\frac{1}{4}$ pint of liquid. Add this to the yeast.

4 Pour this yeast mixture into the flour and beat well for about 5 minutes until the dough is very smooth.

5 Cover the bowl with a cloth and leave in a warm place until the dough has doubled in size.

6 Turn the dough onto a floured board and knead well.

7 Roll the dough into an oblong and turn it so that the short side is towards you. Spread half the remaining butter and sugar onto the two-thirds of the dough furthest from you [*fig. 11 (1)*].

8 Fold the bottom third of the dough up over the sugared part and the top third down towards you and press the edges together [*fig. 11 (2)*].

9 Half turn the dough and roll it out again, repeating the whole process using the rest of the butter and sugar [*fig. 11 (3)*].

10 Half turn the dough again and roll it out into a square $\frac{1}{2}$ in. thick [*fig. 11 (4)*].

11 Spread the fruit over the dough and roll it up like a Swiss roll, leaving the join underneath.

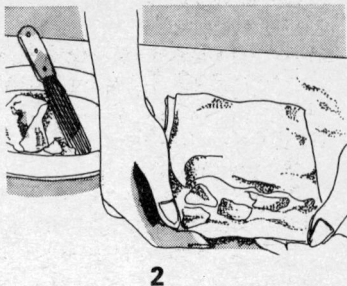

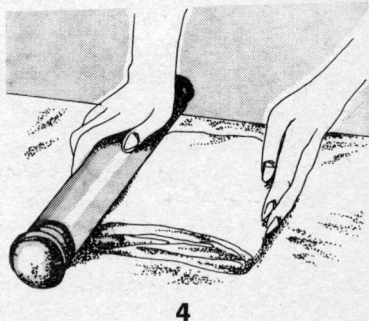

Fig. 11

12 Cut the roll of dough into slices $\frac{1}{2}$ in. thick and put them onto a greased baking tray with the cut side up.

13 Cover the buns up and leave to rise in a warm place until they touch each other (20–30 minutes).

14 Brush them with egg white and sprinkle with sugar. Bake in a hot oven (Gas Mark 6, electric 400°F) for 20 minutes. When they are done, turn them out and separate them while they are still hot.

How to make currant tea cakes

You need: 1 pound plain flour, 1 level teaspoon salt, 1 ounce butter, $\frac{1}{2}$ ounce yeast, $2\frac{1}{2}$ ounces sugar, $\frac{1}{2}$ pint warm milk, 3 ounces currants.

What to do

1 Sift together the flour and salt, rub in the butter until the mixture looks like fine breadcrumbs and put the bowl to warm.

2 Cream the yeast and one teaspoon of sugar until liquid and add half the milk. Leave to stand in a warm place for about 15 minutes.

3 Mix the currants and the rest of the sugar into the flour.

4 Add the yeast mixture to the flour and beat into a soft dough, adding more milk if necessary.

5 Cover the bowl and leave in a warm place until the dough has doubled in size.

6 Turn onto a floured board and divide into nine equal pieces. Knead each piece into a round cake, flatten the tops and place on a greased baking tray.

7 Cover and leave in a warm place for about 15 minutes until they have doubled in size.

8 Bake in a hot oven (Gas Mark 6, electric 400°F) for 10 minutes.

PROJECT

Make rum babas (*fig. 12*)

These are something of a luxury dish but no more difficult to make than any other cake needing yeast. Babas can be eaten either hot or cold, on their own or decorated with whipped cream in the centre. To make them, you need either one large ring mould (a metal jelly mould will do) or one small one for each person. It is important to prepare the mould carefully. This

Fig. 12

recipe needs a mould about 8 in. across, (or six small moulds), and the inside should be brushed all over with melted butter and then lightly sprinkled with flour.

You need: 6 ounces flour, $\frac{1}{2}$ level teaspoon salt, $\frac{1}{2}$ ounce yeast, $1\frac{1}{2}$ ounces sugar, 2 eggs, $2\frac{1}{2}$ ounces *melted* butter, a little milk, grated lemon rind, 2 ounces raisins soaked in rum. *For the syrup:* 4 ounces sugar, $\frac{1}{3}$ pint water, $\frac{1}{4}$ pint rum.

What to do

1 Put the raisins to soak in a little rum.

2 Sift together the flour and salt and warm the bowl.

3 Cream the yeast with a teaspoonful of the sugar and add about a tablespoon of warm milk.

4 Make a well in the centre of the flour and pour in the yeast mixture. Sprinkle flour over the yeast and leave in a warm place for about 10 minutes until the yeast is bubbling through the flour.

5 Mix all the flour and yeast together, add the lightly beaten eggs and enough warm milk to make a light, smooth dough. Beat thoroughly.

6 Cover the bowl with a cloth and leave in a warm place until the dough has doubled in size.

7 Add the warm melted butter and the sugar and beat until the dough is smooth and no longer sticky.

8 Drain the raisins and work them and the lemon peel into the dough.

9 Fill the prepared mould half full of dough and cover it and leave it in a warm place, until the dough rises to the top of the mould.

10 Cover the mould with kitchen foil and bake in a hot oven (Gas Mark 5, electric 375°F) for about 40 minutes.

11 While the baba is cooking, make the syrup by bringing the water and sugar to the boil. Take the pan off the heat and add the rum. Keep the syrup warm but do not let it boil again.

12 When the baba is done, and while it is still hot, turn it out of the mould into a dish and prick it all over with a fork.

13 Pour the syrup over the baba. Scoop up any syrup which runs out and pour it back over the baba until all the syrup is absorbed.

For special occasions the centre of the baba can be filled with whipped cream and decorated with chopped nuts or crystallised fruit.

PART FOUR

Baking cakes

Just like bread, most cakes have to rise to make them look attractive and taste light when they are eaten. If you have ever seen or tasted a cake which has not risen enough in the oven, you will know that it looks and tastes very sad indeed. It is soggy in the middle instead of firm and light. Often, if it has fruit in it, the fruit is in a soggy layer on the bottom of the cake, instead of being spread through the mixture evenly. So you will agree that one of the most important things about making a cake is being sure that it rises in the oven just the right amount.

Cakes rise for the same reason as bread, because of the bubble of gas which we put into the mixture. When the bubbles are heated they grow even bigger and so the mixture rises in its tin before it sets into solid cake. But, in making cakes, we do not use yeast to make the gas bubbles. There are two other methods which are more commonly used for cake making.

Beating in air. If you have ever seen meringues being made you will know that the white part of eggs will hold very many bubbles of air. In fact, eggs are one of the best ways of putting air bubbles into a mixture. This is why it is very important to beat ingredients very thoroughly when you add them to your main cake mixture. The more bubbles you can beat into your eggs and your sugar and butter the lighter your cake will be.

Baking powder. The other way to make a cake mixture rise, is to add baking powder. This is a mixture of bicarbonate of soda and cream of tartar, specially prepared for baking. When these two chemicals are moist and warm, as they are in a cake mixture in the oven, they react together to make little bubbles of carbon dioxide (the same gas yeast makes), and these bubbles do the same job as air bubbles in egg. They rise up and take the rest of the cake mixture with them, making it light and much nicer to eat.

Self-raising flour. Self-raising flour is flour which has baking powder already added. In most recipes self-raising flour is normally used but for some, especially for heavy fruit cakes, it is more satisfactory to use plain flour and add a smaller proportion of baking powder.

OTHER POINTS TO REMEMBER

1 If you are using beaten egg, butter and sugar to make a cake

Fig. 13

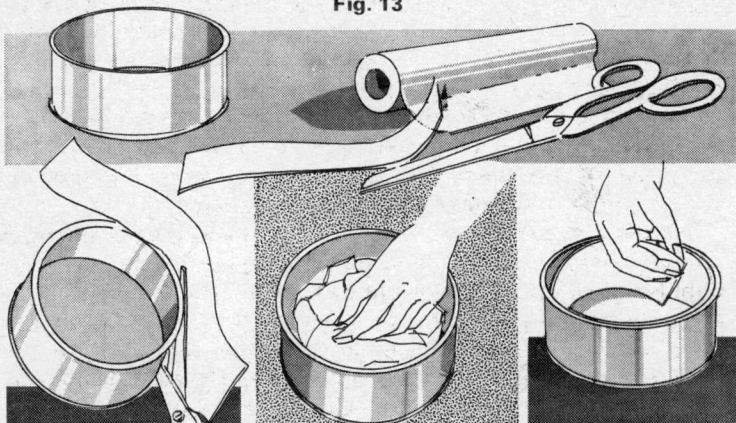

rise, you should be careful not to beat the mixture too much, once you have added the other ingredients. Beat the egg thoroughly on its own. Once it is part of another mixture you should treat it gently. You are more likely to be beating the air bubbles *OUT* than adding any more.

2 Always grease your tins thoroughly before you start making a cake mixture. Tins for sponge cakes made without butter should be greased and sugared. Tins for rich, heavy cakes which cook for a long time should be lined with silicone paper, bottom and sides, or with buttered greaseproof paper (*fig. 13*).

3 Follow the recipe carefully and weigh all the ingredients. The proportions of one ingredient to another are important in cake making.

4 Cakes do not like draughts while they are cooking. *Do not open* the oven door until you are sure the cake is almost done, and *never slam it shut*.

5 Test a cake with a clean knitting needle. If it comes out cleanly the cake is done. If it is sticky, the cake needs a little longer.

PROJECT

Make an egg sponge cake

This is a very light sponge mixture which rises because of the amount of air bubbles you beat into the eggs. So be sure to beat the mixture very thoroughly indeed.

You need: 3 eggs, 4 ounces caster sugar, 4 ounces self-raising flour, jam.

What to do

1 Grease two 7 in. sandwich cake tins and sprinkle the inside with flour and sugar.

2 Put the eggs and sugar into a mixing bowl and put the bowl over a pan of warm, but not boiling water.

3 Keeping the bowl warm over the water, whisk the eggs and sugar together until they are sufficiently thick and creamy for the whisk to leave a trail when it is dragged through the mixture. This may take up to 15 minutes. Use an electric hand whisk if you have one.

4 Sieve the flour and fold it very gently into the egg mixture.

5 Pour the cake mixture into the prepared tins and sprinkle a little sugar on the top.

6 Bake in a moderate oven (Gas Mark 5, electric 375°F) for about 25 minutes. When cold, sandwich the cakes together with jam.

PROJECT

Small sponge cakes

What to do

1 Prepare a set of patty pans by greasing them and sprinkling them with a mixture of flour and sugar.

2 Make a sponge cake mixture according to the previous recipe.

3 Put a spoonful of the mixture into each patty pan and sprinkle a little sugar on the top.

4 Bake in a hot oven (Gas Mark 6, electric 400°F) for about 10 minutes, until they are firm and light brown in colour.

5 Allow the cakes to cool on a wire rack, then slit them in two and fill with jam and whipped cream.

PROJECT

Make a Victoria sandwich

This is a second basic cake recipe, which relies for its lightness partly on the air you can beat into the sugar and butter mixture and into the eggs. So make sure that you beat the sugar and butter until they are very light and fluffy.

You need: 4 ounces butter, 4 ounces caster sugar, 4 ounces self-raising flour, 2 eggs, pinch of salt.

What to do

1 Grease two 7 in. sandwich tins and line the bottom with greaseproof or silicone paper.

2 Put the butter and sugar into a mixing bowl and beat them together until they turn pale in colour and look light and fluffy. This is known as 'creaming' the butter and sugar.

3 Whisk up the eggs in another bowl.

4 Add a little of the egg to the butter mixture and mix in thoroughly. Keep on adding the egg, a little at a time, until it is all mixed in.

5 Add the flour and salt and lightly stir together.

6 Divide the mixture between the cake tins.

7 Bake in a moderate oven (Gas Mark 4, electric 350°F) for about 30 minutes.

Variations

1 Victoria sandwich. This cake can also be sandwiched and filled with jam and whipped cream.

2 Small sponge cakes. You can either use this mixture to make small round cakes, baked in patty pans, as described in the previous project, or bake the mixture in a flat baking tray, (a meat tin would do), and when it is cool cut it up into interesting shapes which can then be iced and decorated.

3 Chocolate cake. To make a chocolate sponge follow the Victoria sponge recipe, but use only $3\frac{1}{2}$ ounces of self-raising flour and add $\frac{1}{2}$ ounce of cocoa powder, mixed in well with the flour.

PART FIVE

Other cakes to bake

This section of the project book includes recipes for many different kinds of simple cake, from a Swiss Roll to Yorkshire Parkin. The recipes are rather more complicated than the simple sponge cake recipes, so read each one carefully, before you start work.

PROJECT

Make a Swiss roll (*fig. 14*)

You need: 3 eggs, 4 ounces caster sugar, 3 ounces self-raising flour, $\frac{1}{2}$ teaspoonful vanilla essence, 1 or 2 tablespoonful warm water, 2 tablespoonsful heated jam.

What to do

1 Grease a Swiss roll tin (about 12 in. by 9 in.) and line it with silicone paper or greaseproof paper.

2 Put the eggs and sugar into a mixing bowl and put the bowl over a pan of warm, but not boiling, water.

3 Keeping the bowl warm over the water, whisk the eggs and sugar together until they are sufficiently thick and creamy for the whisk to leave a trail when it is dragged through the mixture.

4 Add the vanilla essence.

31

Fig. 14

5 Sieve the flour and add it to the mixture, folding it in gently.

6 Add enough of the warm water to make the mixture pour out easily.

7 Pour the mixture into the tin, making sure it fills the corners.

8 Bake in a hot oven (Gas Mark 7, electric 425°F) for 7 to 10 minutes until it is light brown in colour.

9 Spread a sheet of silicone or greaseproof paper out flat and sprinkle it with sugar.

10 Turn the Swiss roll onto the sugared paper and cover it with a clean cloth to cool slightly.

11 Cut off the edges of the roll if they are crisp or discoloured.

12 Warm the jam and spread it over the roll while it is still warm.

13 Start to roll up the Swiss roll by turning the long edge furthest away from you over about $\frac{1}{2}$ in. Press this down firmly and then roll it in towards you with the palms of your hands. Put it on a serving plate with the edge underneath.

Variation

Chocolate roll Follow the Swiss roll recipe but add $\frac{1}{2}$ ounce of cocoa powder with the flour, and use a little extra warm water to make the mixture pour easily. A chocolate roll should be filled with chocolate butter cream and can be iced with chocolate icing. See the projects in Part Six for details.

PROJECT

Make rock buns

You need: 8 ounces self-raising flour, 4 ounces butter, 2 ounces sugar, pinch of salt, 3 ounces currants, 1 ounce chopped candied peel, pinch of mixed spice or nutmeg, 1 egg, $\frac{1}{2}$ cup of milk.

What to do

1 Grease a flat baking tray.

2 Put the flour, salt and butter into a mixing bowl and rub the butter in until the mixture looks like fine breadcrumbs.

3 Add the sugar, currants, candied peel and spice.

4 Mix the egg with a little milk in another bowl.

5 Add the liquid to the flour and mix into a smooth mixture.

6 Spoon the mixture into rough heaps on the baking tray, spacing them evenly.

7 Bake in a hot oven (Gas Mark 6, electric 400°F) for about 20 minutes.

Fig. 15

PROJECT

Make raspberry buns (*fig. 15*)

You need: 8 ounces self-raising flour, 2 ounces sugar, a cup of milk, 3 ounces butter, 1 egg, pinch of salt, raspberry jam.

What to do

1 Grease a flat baking tray.

2 Put the flour and salt into a mixing bowl and rub the butter in until the mixture looks like fine breadcrumbs.

3 Add the sugar and mix in.

4 Whisk the eggs in another bowl and add to the flour mixture.

5 Add just enough milk to make a slightly sticky dough. You may not need a whole cupful.

6 Cut the dough into 8 small pieces and with floury hands roll each piece into a round ball.

7 Make a hole in the centre of each ball with your fingers and fill it with $\frac{1}{4}$ teaspoon of raspberry jam. Close up the balls so that the jam is completely enclosed and place the buns upside down on the tray.

8 Brush the top of each bun with water and sprinkle with a little sugar.

9 Bake in a hot oven (Gas Mark 7, electric 425°F) for about 20 minutes.

PROJECT

Make Yorkshire parkin

You need: 8 ounces self-raising flour, 8 ounces medium oatmeal, 4 ounces sugar, 3 ounces butter, 8 ounces syrup, $\frac{1}{4}$ level teaspoon salt, $\frac{1}{2}$ level teaspoon ground ginger, $\frac{1}{4}$ pint milk.

What to do

1 Grease a baking tin and line it with silicone or greaseproof paper. The best sort is an oblong tin 11 in. by 9 in. and at least 2 in. deep but you can use a round cake tin.

2 Mix the flour, salt, ginger and oatmeal together in a bowl.

3 Put the sugar, butter, syrup and half the milk in a pan and melt them without bringing them to the boil. Then allow the mixture to cool slightly.

4 Add the melted ingredients to the flour and stir thoroughly.

5 Add the rest of the milk and stir in quickly, and pour into the tin.

6 Bake for 1 hour and 20 minutes in a cool oven (Gas Mark 2, electric 300°F).

Parkin will keep for two weeks or more in an airtight tin. In any case it is better to eat it the day *after* baking.

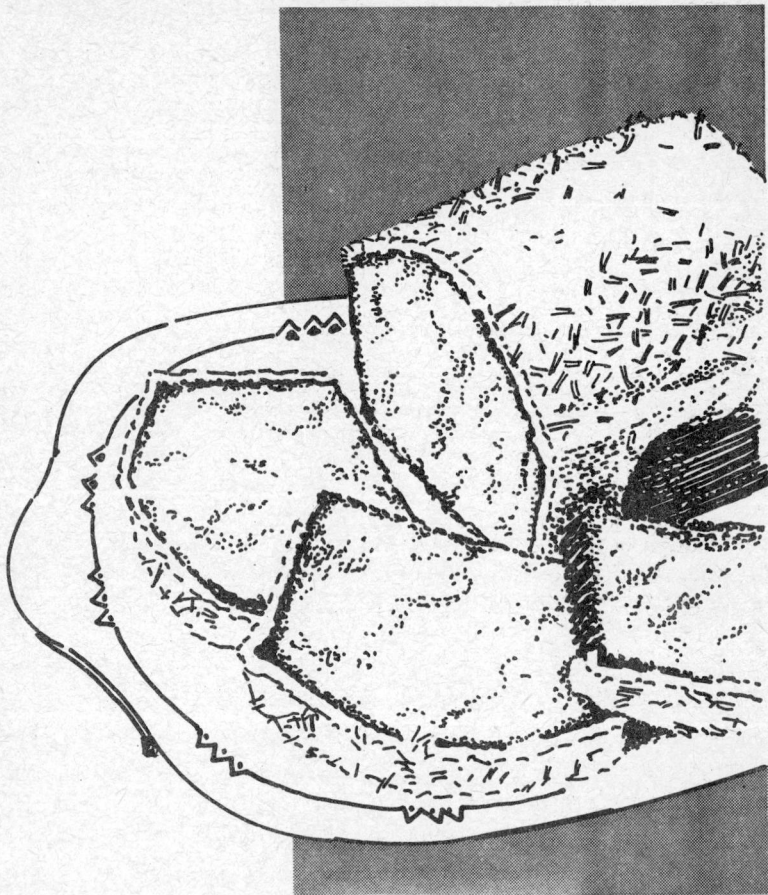

Fig. 16

Coconut cake (*fig. 16*)

You need: 4 ounces butter, 4 ounces sugar, 3 eggs, 7 ounces self-raising flour, 2 ounces dessicated coconut, $\frac{1}{4}$ level teaspoon of salt.

What to do

1 Grease a deep 6 in. cake tin and line it with silicone or greaseproof paper.

2 Put the butter and sugar into a mixing bowl and beat them together until they turn pale in colour and look fluffy.

3 Add the eggs to the mixture one at a time and beat them in.

4 Add the flour, salt and coconut and stir in.

5 Pour the mixture into the prepared cake tin and bake for $1\frac{1}{4}$ hours in a moderate oven (Gas Mark 4, electric 350°F).

6 Decorate the cake by icing it with white icing (see the project in Part Six). Sprinkle dessicated coconut onto the icing while it is still wet.

Variation

Small coconut buns. Use the cake mixture to make small buns baked in patty pans. Decorate half the buns with coconut sprinkled on top before they are baked. This will be toasted in the oven. Ice the rest of the buns and sprinkle with coconut while the icing is wet.

Icings and fillings

Half the fun of making cakes is to vary them, by changing the flavour and the look of them with icings and fillings. This section of the book will tell you how to make various types of icing, and lots of interesting fillings and decorations for cakes. Obviously you will want to make a chocolate filling and icing for your chocolate cake, but have you ever tried chocolate cake with a delicious mocha filling? Have you used your basic sponge cake recipe to make a variety of shapes which can be iced and decorated in a variety of different ways? This section does not aim to tell you what to do. It is simply to give you so many ideas so that you will be able to make a different type of cake every time you bake. There is almost no limit to the combinations you can try, by using this section, and then going on to search for other variations in other recipe books.

Flavourings and colourings

Cooks use flavourings and colourings for cake decorations rather like artists use a palette of paints. In fact, if you buy a set of culinary colours you can regard them very much as paints when you are icing and decorating cakes. They normally come in sets of four (red, yellow, blue and green) and from these you can make any colour in the rainbow. Flavourings can be added in two ways. Either from a bottle of essence, the most common types are almond, vanilla, lemon and coffee, or by adding an ordinary food with the required flavour. In this way you can make coffee-butter cream, either with coffee powder or with coffee essence, or a lemon-flavoured cake either with grated

Fig. 17

lemon rind or with lemon essence. As your cooking progresses you will probably build up a collection of colourings and flavourings, because they are items you normally use only a drop at a time.

PROJECT

Make glacé icing

This is a plain icing for everyday cakes and fancies which can be coloured and flavoured in any way you choose. (Do not use cocoa or coffee *powder* in icing as it will give a speckled appearance. There is a recipe for chocolate icing later in this section.)

You need: icing sugar, lukewarm water, colourings etc.
What to do
1 Sieve the icing sugar into a basin and mix in the water, a

few drops at a time, until it is smooth and will spread easily on top of a cake.

2 If necessary, add flavouring and colouring, or divide the icing up to make several different flavours and colours.

3 If the icing becomes stiff before you have finished coating your cakes warm the bowl gently in a pan of hot water.

PROJECT   Make Royal icing

This is the richer icing which sets hard and is normally used for heavy fruit cakes such as Christmas and wedding cakes. Normally a cake to be coated with Royal icing is first coated with almond paste, (see the following recipe), and the icing is piped into an elaborate decoration. Cake decoration of this kind is dealt with in the last section of this book.

You need: 1 pound of icing sugar, 1 teaspoonful lemon juice, whites of two eggs, a few drops of blue colouring (optional), 1 dessertspoonful of glycerine (optional).

(The blue colouring will prevent the icing going yellow if it is kept for any length of time and the glycerine will prevent it from becoming brittle. It is advisable to use glycerine if you plan to do any elaborate decorations with the icing as it will make them less likely to break.)

What to do
1 Sieve the icing sugar into a bowl.

2 Mix the lemon juice and egg whites in another bowl and gradually add the icing sugar.

3 Beat with a wooden spoon for about 10 to 15 minutes until the icing is smooth and white. Add colouring and glycerine. The icing should be stiff enough to hold the spoon standing in it.

4 Smooth the icing over the cake, using a knife dipped into hot water. If you want to keep some of the icing for decoration or for a different colouring to be added later, keep it in a bowl covered with a damp cloth.

PROJECT   Make almond paste

You need: 6 ounces icing sugar, and 6 ounces caster sugar (OR 12 ounces icing sugar), 12 ounces ground almonds, 1 teaspoonful lemon juice, $\frac{1}{2}$ teaspoonful almond essence, 1 or 2 eggs (you can use either the whole eggs, or just the yolks or just the whites. The yolks alone, give a richer, more yellow paste. Whites alone, make a rather brittle paste. If you are using egg whites for Royal icing then you can use the yolks for almond paste.)

What to do
1 Sieve the icing sugar into a bowl and mix in the ground almonds and caster sugar.
2 Add the lemon juice, essence and enough egg to bind the ingredients together into a dry paste which can be moulded in the fingers.
3 Knead the paste thoroughly in the hands until it is smooth.
4 To cover a cake, roll the paste out on a sugared board until it makes a circle about 4 in. wider than the top of the cake [*fig. 18 (1)*].
5 Brush the cake all over with warm apricot jam.
6 Place the cake upside down onto the almond paste circle.
7 Work the paste with your hands until it comes almost to the bottom edge of the cake (the side nearest to you) [*fig. 18 (2)*].
8 Use a straight-side jar or glass to roll around the sides of the cake to make them as smooth as possible. Keep smoothing until the sides are firm and straight and the top edges of the cake are sharp and smooth [*fig. 18 (3)*].
A cake covered with almond paste should be left for several

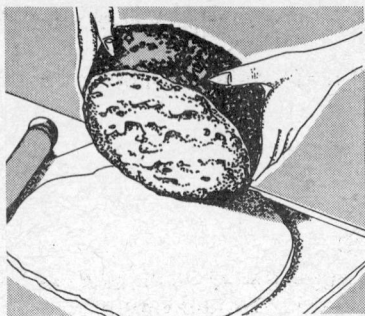

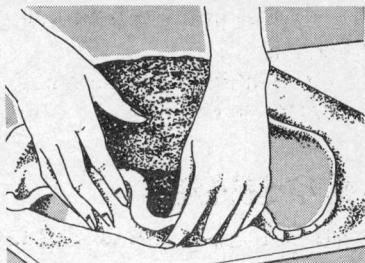

Fig. 18

days to dry before it is iced, because the oil from the paste may discolour the icing.

<h2>PROJECT</h2>

Make chocolate icing

You need: 1 ounce chocolate, 1 tablespoonful water, 4 ounces icing sugar, $\frac{1}{2}$ ounce butter, vanilla or rum essence.

What to do

1 Put the chocolate and the water into a pan and melt the chocolate *very slowly*.

2 Beat in the icing sugar until the icing is thick enough to spread.

3 Beat in the butter and a drop of essence and use the icing immediately.

PROJECT

Make mocha filling and icing

This is a filling which can be used either to fill or ice a cake. It goes well with a coffee or chocolate flavoured sponge.

You need: 3 ounces butter, 6 ounces icing sugar, 2 table-spoonsful cocoa powder, 1 teaspoonful vanilla essence, 1 cupful strong black coffee.

What to do

1 Mix the sugar and cocoa and add them to the fat. Cream them together until they are light and fluffy.

2 Add the essence and then the black coffee until the icing is thin enough to spread. Use the icing immediately.

How to make butter cream

This is a basic cream which can be used to fill or decorate cakes. It can be coloured or flavoured as you wish.

You need: 6 ounces icing sugar (*or* 3 ounces icing sugar and 3 ounces caster sugar), 3 ounces butter, flavouring and/or colouring.

What to do

1 Mix the sugar and butter in a bowl and beat them together until they are light and fluffy.

2 Add any colouring or flavouring and use to fill or decorate cakes. (You can use coffee and cocoa powder in butter cream as flavouring.)

PART SEVEN

More elaborate cakes

This section of the book deals with more elaborate cakes, some of them from other parts of the world. If you go to the Continent, you will see many well-stocked cake shops in most European countries. Many of the cakes they make use ground almonds, and the recipe for Japs in this section, is typical of these. Many European countries also specialise in cheesecakes. The recipe given here is for a Polish cheesecake, but you will also find similar cakes in Austria, and many countries of Eastern Europe. Angel cake and strawberry shortcake are favourites in America, and apple cakes are found, in one form or another, in many European countries. Meringues are a favourite almost everywhere. When you have tried these recipes you may be able to find others from other foreign countries. Almost every country has at least one cake which is especially popular.

PROJECT

Make meringues (*fig. 20*)

It is important to cook meringues so that they do not stick to the baking tray. Either cook them on a layer of rice paper which is edible, or use silicone paper to prevent them sticking. Grease-

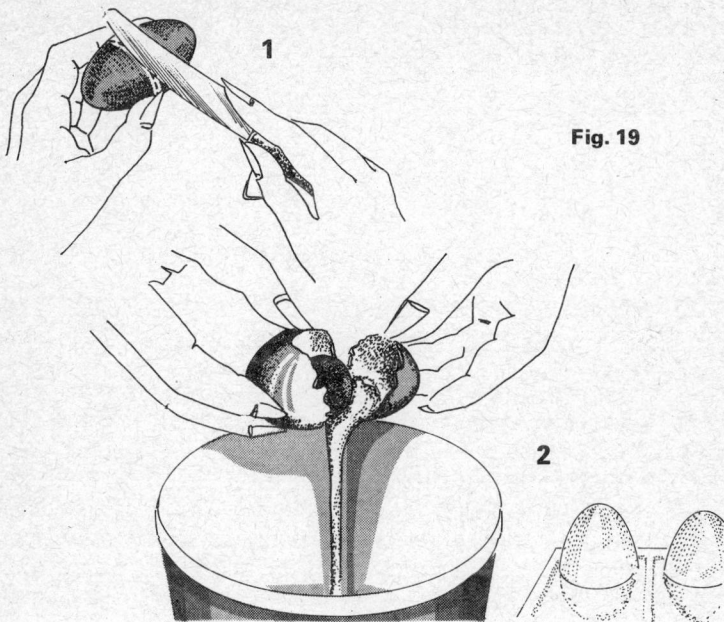

Fig. 19

proof paper is *not* suitable. *Fig. 19 (1) and (2)* shows how to separate egg whites from yolks.

You need: 2 egg whites, pinch of salt, 4 ounces caster sugar, $\frac{1}{4}$ pint whipped cream.

What to do

1 Place the egg whites and the salt in a clean, dry bowl and whisk them until the egg stands up in stiff points.

2 Beat in two or three teaspoonfuls of sugar.

3 Fold in the rest of the sugar very gently.

Fig. 20

4 Either spoon the mixture onto the lined baking tray in an even number of heaps, or pipe it through a forcing bag into shell shapes.

5 Sprinkle caster sugar over the shapes and bake in a very cool oven (Gas Mark $\frac{1}{2}$, electric 250°F) until the meringues are firm.

6 Loosen the meringues and press in the soft centre. Return them to the oven to dry out completely.

7 When the meringues are cool sandwich two together with thick whipped cream.

PROJECT   Make japs

You need: 2 egg whites, 4 ounces caster sugar, 4 ounces ground almonds, almond essence, glacé icing, coffee flavoured butter cream.

What to do

1 Grease and flour a baking tray.

2 Whisk the egg whites until they are stiff and whisk in half the sugar.

3 Fold in the ground almonds, a few drops of essence and the rest of the sugar very lightly.

4 Spread the mixture evenly, about $\frac{1}{2}$ in. deep, over the baking tray and bake in a moderate oven (Gas Mark 4, electric 350°F) until almost set.

5 Remove the tray from the oven and cut the mixture into rounds with a $1\frac{1}{2}$ in. pastry cutter. Return them to the oven with the bits you have trimmed off and take them out to cool when they are quite firm. Leave the trimmings to cook until they are a deep golden colour.

6 When the trimmings are cold crush them with a rolling pin and pass them through a fine sieve.

7 Sandwich the rounds together in pairs with butter cream and spread the top and sides with butter cream. Coat them completely with the sieved crumbs which should stick to the cream easily.

8 Make the cakes neat with the blade of a knife and you may, if you like, decorate the top of each with a little icing of any colour or flavour you like.

PROJECT

Make American angel cake

You need: 2 ounces flour, $4\frac{1}{2}$ ounces caster sugar, 6 egg whites, pinch of salt, $\frac{1}{2}$ teaspoonful cream of tartar, $\frac{1}{2}$ teaspoonful vanilla essence.

What to do

1 Flour a 6 in. cake tin without greasing it.

2 Sift the flour and sugar separately at least three times, then sift $\frac{1}{4}$ of the sugar with all the flour.

3 Whisk the egg whites until frothy, sprinkle in the cream of tartar and continue whisking until the egg stands up in stiff points.

4 Lightly beat in the sugar and a few drops of essence.

5 Fold in the sugar and flour mixture very gently a little at a time.

6 Pour the mixture into a tin and bake in a very cool oven (Gas Mark 3, electric 325°F) for 45 minutes.

7 Allow the cake to cool in its tin turned upside down for about 30 minutes before turning out. Angel cake can be iced, dusted with icing sugar or served with tinned or soft fresh fruit and whipped cream.

PROJECT Make Polish cheesecake

You need: For the pastry, 8 ounces plain flour, 4 ounces butter, pinch of salt, water.

For the filling, $\frac{1}{2}$ pound cottage cheese, 3 ounces sugar, 2 eggs, 1 ounce butter, vanilla essence, juice and grated rind of half a lemon, a few sultanas.

What to do

1 *The pastry.* Put the flour, salt and butter into a bowl and rub until the mixture looks like fine breadcrumbs.

2 Add enough water to make a fairly dry dough.

3 Roll out the pastry thinly and line a 9 in. greased cake tin at least 1 in. deep.

4 *The filling.* Melt the butter and stir it into the cheese.

5 Separate the egg yolks from the whites and add the yolks, sugar, lemon rind and juice and a few drops of vanilla essence to the cheese and mix in thoroughly.

6 Whisk the egg whites until they are stiff and fold gently into the cheese mixture.

7 Sprinkle a few sultanas onto the pastry crust and pour in the filling.

8 Bake in a hot oven (Gas Mark 7, electric 425°F) for 10 minutes and then reduce the heat to Gas Mark 4, electric 350°F and bake for another 30 minutes.

Make American strawberry shortcake (*fig. 21*)

You need: 8 ounces self-raising flour, ½ ounce ground almonds, pinch of salt, 4½ ounces butter, 2 ounces sugar, 1 egg yolk, ½ pound (or more) strawberries, sugar, whipped cream.

What to do

1 Mix the flour, salt and ground almonds together in a bowl.

2 Cream the butter and sugar together until they are light and fluffy and add the egg yolk.

3 Using your hand or a wooden spoon gradually work the flour mixture into the butter until it makes a firm dough.

Fig. 21

4 Divide the dough into three equal pieces and roll each one out into a round at least $\frac{1}{4}$ in. thick. Bake in a moderate oven (Gas Mark 4, electric 350°F) on a flat baking tray until golden brown. Then allow to cool.

5 Crush the strawberries slightly to let out a little juice, add sugar and a little cream and mix in well.

6 Spread strawberries onto a layer of shortcake, put another layer of shortcake on top and then more strawberries to make a *three-decker* sandwich, finishing off with a layer of strawberries.

7 Pipe or spoon whipped cream on top and round the edges and decorate.

PROJECT

Make Austrian apple strudel (*fig. 22*)

You need: For the pastry, 6 ounces flour, 4 ounces butter, 2 ounces caster sugar, milk to mix.

For the filling, $1\frac{1}{2}$ pounds cooking apples, 2 ounces sultanas, 2/3 ounces sugar, $\frac{1}{2}$ level teaspoonful mixed spice, 2 tablespoonsful breadcrumbs.

What to do

1 *The pastry.* Sift the flour and sugar into a bowl with the butter and rub them together until the mixture looks like fine breadcrumbs.

2 Add just enough milk to make a dry dough.

3 Roll the pastry out thinly into an oblong shape and place it on a greased baking tray.

4 *The filling.* Peel, core and slice the apples thinly and mix them with the sugar, spice and breadcrumbs.

5 Pile the apple filling into the centre of the pastry and fold the two ends over so that they almost meet and cover the apple.

6 Brush the pastry with milk and bake in a moderate oven (Gas Mark 6, electric 400°F) for 20 to 30 minutes. To serve, cut into thick slices and dust with icing sugar.

Fig. 22

PART EIGHT

Fruit cakes

Fruit cakes are richer than sponge cakes and these mixtures are usually chosen for special occasions, for birthdays, for Christmas and for weddings. They can be eaten plain, but are more often decorated with almond paste and icing. This section will give you recipes for every-day fruit cakes and also very rich recipes, which can be used for special occasions. Some cooks feel that fruit cakes are more difficult to make than plain cakes, but this need not be so, if a few simple precautions are taken with the preparations.

Preparing the fruit

Because dried fruit is heavy, it can sink to the bottom of a cake mixture making the cake look very uneven when it is sliced. Always wash dried fruit before use, but make sure that it is completely dry before you add it to the cake mixture. Wet fruit is more likely to sink. You can make sure it is dry by leaving it in the oven for ten minutes, with the oven door open, before you start baking.

Crystallised fruit, such as glacé cherries and candied peel can also be added to fruit cakes. Glacé cherries are rather large and heavy so they should be chopped into quarters before they are added to the mixture. Any surplus sugar should be removed from candied peel, which should also be chopped. If the crystallised fruit is sticky, it can be tossed in a little of the flour, which you have weighed for your mixture, and this will help to keep the pieces apart.

The mixture

A fruit cake mixture is generally very thick so that it can support the heavy fruit. The spoon should stand up in the mixture which may be difficult to transfer to the baking tin. Make sure that all the corners of a square cake tin are filled with mixture.

Tins

Tins for baking fruit cakes should be *well lined* and *greased* as the cakes bake very slowly. If the tin is not well lined, the crust of the cake will burn before the centre is cooked. Fruit cakes can be made in round or square tins, or even in a loaf tin. Wedding cakes normally have two or three tiers, made in tins of different sizes, and balanced one on top of the other after they have been iced and decorated.

Flour

Most rich fruit cakes are made by the creaming method which means that air is beaten into the mixture of fat, sugar and eggs. This is usually sufficient to make the cake rise and very little baking powder is needed to help the rising process. For this reason, it is better not to use self-raising flour for fruit cakes. Use plain flour and follow the instructions for the amount of baking powder needed very carefully.

Fig. 23

Make a Dundee cake (*fig. 23*)

You need: 6 ounces butter, 6 ounces caster sugar, 3 eggs, 8 ounces plain flour, $\frac{1}{4}$ level teaspoonful salt, 1 level teaspoonful baking powder, $\frac{1}{2}$ level teaspoonful ground cinnamon, pinch of grated nutmeg, grated rind of a lemon, 6 ounces currants, 3 ounces raisins, 4 ounces sultanas, 2 ounces candied peel, 2 ounces blanched almonds, a little milk.

What to do

1 Grease and line a 7 in. deep cake tin.

2 Cream the butter and sugar until they are pale in colour and fluffy.

3 Beat the eggs thoroughly, and gradually beat into the mixture.

4 Sift the flour, salt and baking powder together and mix the fruit with a small amount of the flour.

5 Chop half the almonds.

6 Mix in the flour, fruit, lemon rind and the chopped almonds. If necessary, add a little milk, but the mixture should be stiff enough for the spoon to stand upright.

7 Spoon the mixture into the baking tin and arrange the rest of the almonds in a design on the top.

8 Bake in a moderate oven (Gas Mark 4, electric 350°F) for 45 minutes, then reduce the heat to Gas Mark 3, electric 325°F and bake for another hour and a half.

PROJECT Make a birthday cake

You need: 4 ounces butter, 4 ounces moist brown sugar, 1½ ounces golden syrup, 2 eggs, 6 ounces plain flour, ¼ level teaspoonful salt, 1 level teaspoonful baking powder, 11 ounces mixed fruit (currants, sultanas, glacé cherries etc.), 2 ounces candied peel, a little milk.

What to do

1 Grease and line a 6 or 7 in. deep cake tin.

2 Cream the butter, sugar and syrup until they are light and fluffy.

3 Sift the flour, salt and baking powder together.

4 Whisk the eggs thoroughly.

5 Add the egg little by little to the butter and sugar, beating the mixture well after each addition, then carefully fold in nearly all the flour.

6 Mix the fruit with the remaining flour and then add all the remaining ingredients to the mixture.

7 Mix in enough milk to make a fairly soft mixture and pour into the tin.

8 Bake for 30 minutes in a moderate oven (Gas Mark 4, electric 350°F), Then reduce the heat to Gas Mark 2, electric 300°F, and bake for another 1½ hours.

For projects on cake decoration look at the next section.

PROJECT

Make a Christmas cake

You need: 8 ounces butter, 8 ounces caster sugar, 8 ounces plain flour, a pinch of salt, 1 level teaspoonful mixed spice, $\frac{1}{2}$ level teaspoonful baking powder, 5 eggs, 1 pound currants, 8 ounces raisins, 4 ounces chopped glacé cherries, 2 ounces chopped candied peel, 4 ounces blanched, chopped almonds, a little milk, a little brandy.

What to do

1 Grease and line an 8 in. deep cake tin.

2 Cream the butter and sugar until light and fluffy.

3 Sift together the flour, salt, mixed spice and baking powder.

4 Whisk the eggs thoroughly.

5 Add the egg little by little, beating the mixture well after each addition, then carefully fold in the flour.

6 Stir in the fruit and nuts and, if necessary, add a little milk to make a heavy, smooth mixture.

7 Put the mixture into the tin and make a slight depression in the centre.

8 Bake in a warm oven for 30 minutes (Gas Mark 3, electric 325°F). Then reduce the heat to Gas Mark 1, electric 275°F and bake for another $3\frac{1}{2}$ hours.

9 When the cake is cold, prick the base with a fork and sprinkle 4 or 5 tablespoonfuls of brandy over it. Leave it for a few days before icing.

PART NINE

Cake decoration

Before embarking on this section of the book you need to buy or borrow a set of icing pipes. You will find that these pipes come in different shapes, to form different patterns in the icing, and in different sizes. To do simple cake decoration, it would be reasonable to start with a set of six icing pipes, including at least two sizes of plain pipe to make thin and thick plain lines, a star tube, a shell tube and a basket tube. With these you will be able to make a variety of shapes and patterns including the traditional shell shapes, scrolls and stars or flowers (*fig. 24*).

Making paper piping bags

If you are piping several different colours of icing, it is cheap and convenient to make a piping bag for each colour out of greaseproof or silicone kitchen paper. Cut out a square of paper about 6 in. by 6 in. and roll this up into a neat cone, fold over the top to hold in place, then cut off the sharp end of the cone and fit your icing pipe into the hole.

How to pipe the icing

Make one piping bag for each colour to be used. Fill the bags two thirds full and turn over the edges so that it cannot leak out at the top. Holding the pipe between the first and second fingers

Fig. 24

force the icing out through the pipe by pressing with the thumbs. Start piping at the centre of the cake and work outwards, finishing with the sides and, if the cake is on a board, the base.

OTHER POINTS TO REMEMBER

1 If you are using several colours, always wash the pipes before you change from one colour to another.

2 To do an elaborate cake decoration, it helps if you can obtain a turntable. This makes it much simpler to smooth the icing round the sides of the cake, and to pipe evenly in a circular design on the top of the cake.

3 Plan your design in advance. Never begin a decoration without knowing exactly what you want the cake to look like when it is finished. The best method is to draw your design on a piece of paper before you start. You can then place the paper on top of the cake and prick the design through with a pin.

4 Do not use colours which are too bright. Pastel shades usually look the most attractive. Pink and blue are often used for birthday cakes for small children, but you can experiment with more interesting colour combinations such as apricot and pale green, pink and mauve on birthday cakes. Traditional colours for Christmas decorations include red and green but these should be used sparingly or the cake may look garish. Wedding cakes are normally decorated in white and silver.

Getting in some practise

Before you begin to pipe Royal icing, which is expensive to make and wasted if you spoil your design, why not practise piping with some butter icing made according to the recipe in Part Six. Butter icing can be coloured with culinary colourings and you can use it to ice an ordinary sponge cake. This will give you a clear idea of what you can do with your icing pipes. If your designs do not work the first time, butter icing can be returned to a mixing dish and mixed up again without coming to any harm. You will find that you can make attractive large and small decorated cakes with piped butter icing in various colours and flavours.

PROJECT

Ice a cake with Royal icing

The aim of covering a cake in icing is to make it as smooth as possible as a good base for further decoration. Here are two methods for getting a very smooth finish to your Royal icing. Cakes to be covered with Royal icing should first be covered with almond paste, made according to instructions on page 41, and then left several days for the almond paste to dry out thoroughly.

Method one

1 Place the cake on a cake board (silvered for birthday and wedding cakes).

2 For an 8 in. cake make Royal icing according to the recipe in Part Six using $1\frac{1}{4}$ pounds of icing sugar, mixed to a stiff consistency.

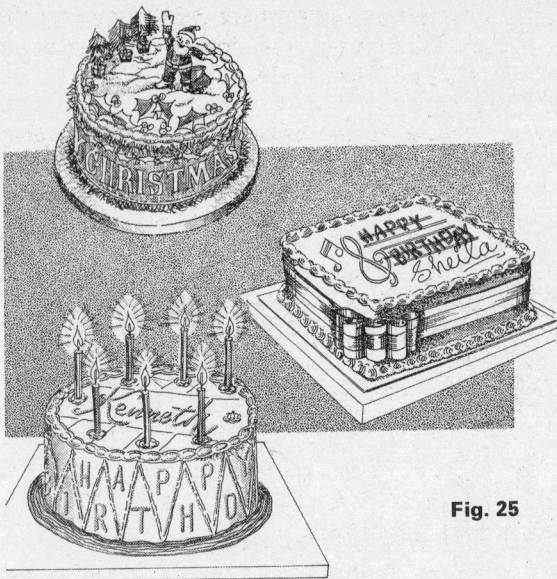

Fig. 25

3 Spoon enough icing to cover the top of the cake into the centre and spread it over the surface with a hot, wet palette knife. To get a completely level surface draw the edge of the palette knife over the surface of the cake towards you in one final sweeping movement.

4 Cover the sides of the cake with icing smoothed on with the palette knife, and finish off (if possible on a turntable) by turning the cake round against the edge of the knife. Smooth off any overlap, which has been pushed over the top edge of the cake.

5 Leave this first coating to dry for several days.

6 Make the second coat of slightly thinner icing using one pound of icing sugar and pour this over the cake so that it runs over the top and down the sides, covering it completely. Allow this coat to set before decorating.

Method two

1 Cover the sides of the cake with thick icing and smooth carefully with a palette knife as in instruction 4, page 60.

2 With a large piping tube, star or shell, pipe a thick decorative pattern round the outer edge of the cake top and allow to dry.

3 Thin the rest of the icing to a pouring consistency and pour it onto the top of the cake. To ensure a glossy surface dry this icing off quickly in an oven left on the lowest possible heat with the door open.

Both these methods can then be used as a basis for decoration.

PROJECT

Decorate a birthday cake (*fig. 25*)

The simplest way to pipe a decoration on a birthday cake is to write Happy Birthday, or some similar greeting on the top of the cake. This can be done in any colour and surrounded by other decorations. To make sure that your greeting will fit the top of the cake, write it out first in the chosen lettering on a piece of transparent tracing or greaseproof paper. This can then be put over the top of the cake to check that it fits. Then the design can be very lightly pricked through the paper onto the basic icing with a pin. This will make piping the greeting very much easier.

FOR FURTHER READING

REFERENCE BOOK

Bakery: Cakes and Simple Confectionery, by Maris Floris. *Michael Joseph,*

KITCHEN COOK BOOKS

Cake Icing and Decorating, by Jean Bowring. *Angus and Robertson,*

Bread and Scones, by Marguerite Patten. *Hamlyn,*

Cake Icing and Decoration, by Marguerite Patten. *Hamlyn,*

Cake Making in Pictures, by Muriel Downes. *Odhams,*

Concerning Cake Making, by Helen Jerome. *Pitman,*

Craft Breadmaking, by J. Sizer. *Maclaren,*

Farmhouse Cakes and Home Baked Bread, by Kathleen Thomas. *Newnes* (**Countrywise Books**),

Home Baked: A Little Book of Bread Recipes, by George and C. Scurfield. *Faber,*

The standard textbook for the trade is **Breadmaking**, by E. B. Bennion, *Oxford University Press,*   (400 pages with 90 illustrations.)

To buy any of the above books, first try your local bookseller. If he does not have it in stock, he will be pleased to order it for you. In case of difficulty, write to the publisher of the book in question.

POSSIBLE CAREERS

BAKING INDUSTRY. Your career would be with firms making bread, cakes and biscuits. Enter as an apprentice at 15 or 16, with day release to study at a technical college, or take two- or three-year full-time or sandwich courses leading to the National Diploma in Baking, for which you need four 'O' levels or C.S.E. Grade 1, including English and Science.

Read: Baking, Choice of Careers Booklet No. 84 (from booksellers or Her Majesty's Stationery Office).

Write to: National Board for Bakery Education, Queen's House, Holly Road, Twickenham, Middlesex, for a list of more books to consult, and further careers information.

CATERING INDUSTRY. Train to become a cook or chef by taking a full-time two-year course at a technical college, or take a job in a hotel or restaurant kitchen, and study part-time on a two- or four-year apprenticeship. There are many other possible careers in the hotel and catering industries. For management, take longer full-time courses at technical colleges or at the Universities of Surrey and Strathclyde.

Read: Management in the Hotel and Catering Industry and **Hotel and Catering Occupations,** Choice of Careers Booklets Nos. 15 and 33 (from booksellers or H.M.S.O.).

Write to: Hotel and Catering Institute, 191 Trinity Road, London S.W.17, for list of colleges offering full-time courses.

DOMESTIC SCIENCE—can cover teaching, demonstrating, catering in industry and institutions such as hospitals and schools, and work in dietetics. You can enter it at various levels, after a short technical-college course requiring no formal educational qualification, after longer courses for which you need 'O' and 'A' level qualifications, after a course for a teacher's diploma, or after a university degree from London or Bristol.

Read: Domestic Science and Dietetics, Choice of Careers Booklet No. 13 (from booksellers or H.M.S.O.).

FOOD MANUFACTURING INDUSTRY. You could find a career at 'O' or 'A' level, or as a graduate in science or arts. Training depends on the qualifications you already hold, but with 'A' level you could do a four-year sandwich course at the National College of Food Technology at Weybridge, Surrey. The Universities of Leeds, Reading, Nottingham and Strathclyde have courses leading to a B.Sc. in Food Science.

Write to: Food Manufacturers' Federation Inc., 4 Lygon Place, London S.W.1.

200

PROJECT BOOKS

continued from
inside front cover